Fish and Shellfish

Myra Street

A QUANTUM BOOK

This book is produced by
Quantum Publishing Ltd.
6 Blundell Street
London N7 9BH

This edition printed 2004

ISBN 1-86160-903-5

QUMFSC-R

Printed in Singapore by
Star Standard Industries Pte Ltd

Contents

INTRODUCTION

It is always fascinating to see that many people will eat fish dishes in restaurants, yet rarely will they prepare the same simple fare at home. Fish is very often best cooked without frills, by grilling, baking or poaching, and no one does more preparation for the consumer than the fish shop! There is very little waste as the bones and heads can be used to make fish stock. It is often the thought of making these stocks which makes fish cookery seem complicated. In fact, they are the work of minutes and greatly enhance the delicate flavor of the fish when cooked; it is generally much quicker to cook fish than meat.

Nowadays there is such a variety of fish available that the choice can be bewildering and many cooks tend to stick to the familiar few. But with a little experiment, great variety can be added to everyday menus. Excellent freezing techniques have made it possible to buy a great selection. Fish is often frozen at sea and therefore extremely fresh if properly stored and thawed.

More expensive fish such as salmon, turbot and halibut are excellent value for money because, being rich, large portions are unnecessary. Shellfish are extremely versatile, highly nutritious and amazingly simple to prepare if you are a novice fish cook. Ask your fish shop for advice and they will usually do all the groundwork for you.

Fish is an excellent source of protein and, as most people are conscious of healthy eating, it is comforting to know that the fat content of fish is highly unsaturated. This means fish, as long as it is not fried, can play a valuable part in providing the protein we need without adding to the cholesterol levels associated with heart disease.

The nutrient content of most fish is made up as follows: 25% protein; 22% fats; 2% minerals and 85% water. White fish have very little fat in the flesh, about 0.5% and in some fish such as haddock or cod, the fat is laid down in the liver. This makes the flesh of white fish particularly valuable in low fat diets. Because the fat is mainly unsaturated, even the oily fish, such as mackerel and herring, are wonderful sources of high-energy food. Recent research suggests that fish oils can help to break down cholesterol in the body. Fish and fish oils are a rich source of vitamins A and D which we all need for glowing health.

The ideal dieter's food usually contains very little carbohydrate and this makes fish suitable for diets. However, calorie counters must sacrifice all those delicious buttery sauces and settle instead for poaching and baking with the addition of lemon juice and fresh herbs. Mind you, this is not such a sacrifice for the end result will be just as tasty. Those on gluten-free and diabetic diets can also enjoy fish providing that no flour products are used in their preparation.

The fish used for recipes in this book are often interchangeable with other similar types of fish. Although classic recipes may seem forbidding, I have simplified where possible and have included many popular favorites which are becoming 'little classics,' especially in the section for appetizers.

Fish appetizers are so popular now for entertaining that fish as a main course is often overlooked, which is a pity. Fish can be ideal as a party main course or the focus of the buffet table. Its delicacy should always be remembered when choosing vegetables and wine. Strong flavors can spoil the taste of the fish.

SELECTION OF FISH

Tomatoes, mushrooms, peas, French beans, broccoli, carrots, leeks and potatoes are all good basic vegetables to serve. Rice with onion, chopped tomato and chopped pepper is delicious too with fish dishes which have a sauce, but rice and fish without a sauce can be rather dry and uninteresting.

The sauce section in the book is important, as many simple dishes have classic sauces served with them and it is these which turn the meal into a feast.

Fish is nutritious and priced competitively in comparison with other high-protein foods, and enables you to produce gourmet meals quickly. There is no reason for people to feel unsure of their abilities to cook any variety of fish dishes. Make a decision today to include more fish dishes in your menus and you will be delighted with the results.

SELECTION

When buying fish and shellfish absolute freshness is essential. Bright eyes and stiff flesh are the signs of fresh fish. Dull eyes and limp flesh with a slight ammonia smell indicate stale fish.

It is best to buy fish the day it is to be cooked. Store it in the refrigerator loosely covered and try not to keep it longer than 24 hours before cooking.

PREPARATION OF FISH

Ideally, fish should be prepared just before cooking but time does not always permit this. If it is to be cooked in a stock it is often advantageous to allow it to cool in the fish liquid.

Most people are not keen on cleaning or gutting fish and it is fortunate that fish shops are so helpful with preparation. However, for those who are prepared to do the work themselves, this is how it should be done.

To scale fish. Lay fish on a piece of kitchen paper and hold by the tail. Scrape scales always from the tail towards the head using the blunt side of a knife. Rinse under cold water.

TO CLEAN AND FILLET FLAT FISH

Slit behind the head on the dark skin side, remove the entrails from the cavity and rinse in cold water. Pat dry with a clean cloth or paper towels. Remove the fins with a sharp knife or scissors.
1 Begin filleting the fish by cutting into head end against the bone.

2 Cut the fillet away carefully with the skin attached to it, leaving the bone as clean as possible.

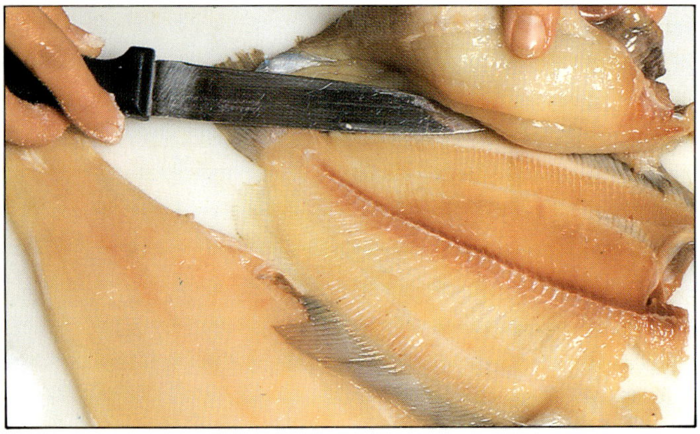

3 Turn the fish over, insert the knife at the head and carefully remove the second fillet in the same way. The flat fish is now filleted. One fillet has thick black skin, the other white skin. The bone can now be used for fish stock.

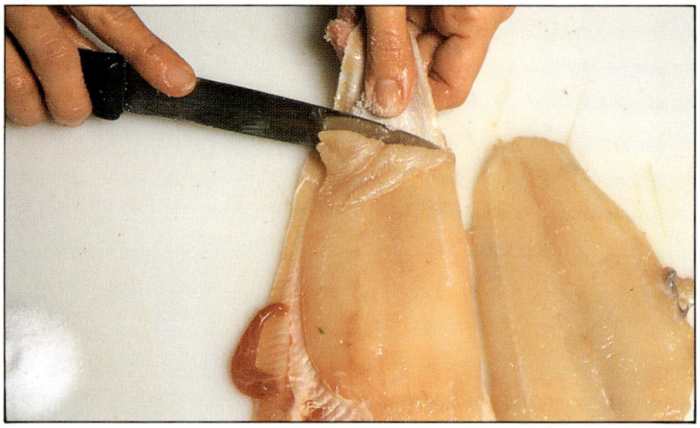

4 To skin the fish, hold the tail firmly and work fillet away from the skin from tail to head, with a sharp knife. The skin can also be used for fish stock.

PREPARATION OF FISH

TO CLEAN AND BONE ROUND FISH

1 If the head is not required as with, for example, mackerel and herring, cut it off with a sharp knife before boning.

2 To clean, retaining the head, slit from under the head down to the tail.

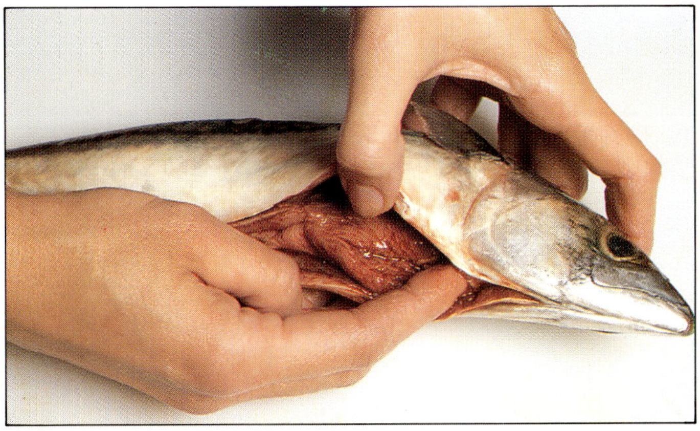

3 Remove entrails by hooking the finger under the throat and pulling down towards the tail. Wash well. A rubber glove may be used for this step.

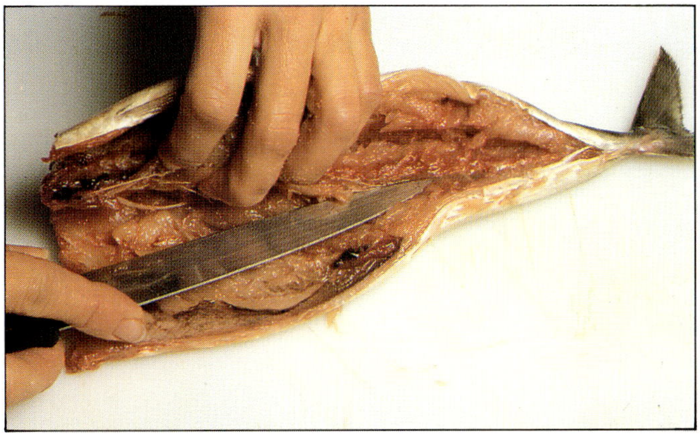

4 Slip the sharp knife under the bone on each side of the fish in turn, open and remove bone.

5 An alternative method which may be easier for the inexperienced is to turn the fish open side downwards. Press down on the back with the heel of the hand to loosen the bone.

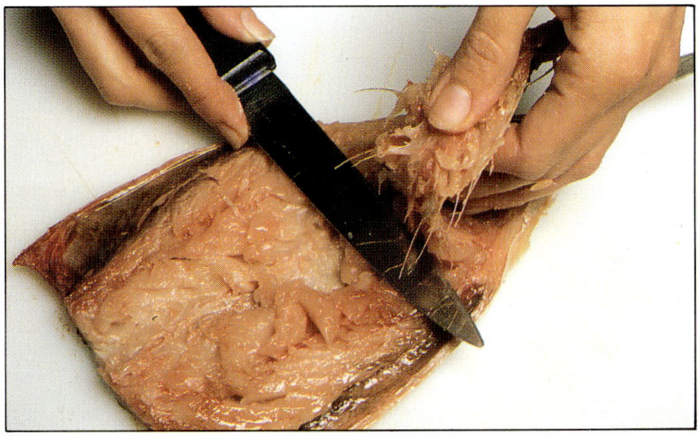

6 Turn the fish over and starting at the tail end, place the blade of the knife under the bone and push along the spine to release. Feel the surface of the fish with the fingers to ensure there are no stray bones. The round fish is now ready to be cooked.

METHODS OF COOKING FISH

BAKING

This method of cookery uses a controlled temperature in an oven. When fat or oil is used the food is said to be roasted. Baking in the oven is suitable for whole fish and fish fillets.

1 Foil and casseroles are often used for baking fish. Baking ensures an even distribution of heat for the complete cooking of fish, or the first stage of a fish dish, which may have a delicious sauce made from the juices left over from the cooking in the oven.

2 Most whole fish are baked at *350°F.*

3 Smaller fish or fillets are usually cooked at around 400°F for a shorter time.

4 Fish should be brushed with a little fat or oil, and usually some liquid such as Court-Bouillon or wine flavored with herbs is added.

BRAISING OR CASSEROLING

This method can be carried out either on top of the stove or in the oven and will include a selection of vegetables, stock or wine with the fish which is cooked in a casserole or ovenproof dish.

1 Remember that the vegetables must be tender at the same time as the fish is cooked. Therefore, it is usually advisable to sweat the vegetables first (by cooking over a low heat) to make sure that they are partially cooked before adding the fish.

2 Large chunks of fish, fish steaks or cutlets can be cooked by this method.

MICROWAVE COOKING

The microwave oven cooks fish very successfully, retaining all the natural moisture and delicacy. It is also an excellent way to reheat dishes to avoid any loss of texture and flavour.

1 Usually it is advisable to cook covered with plastic wrap which has had slits cut.

2 Place the thinner ends of the fish towards the middle of the dish and these can be overlapped if necessary.

3 To cook fish which requires flaking in the recipe, cook until just firm then allow to stand for a few minutes. It will then flake easily.

4 Brush fish such as trout which has the skin left on with butter, otherwise no fat is necessary.

5 If sauce is to be added to the fish in the microwave, it is usually advisable to do this halfway through the cooking process.

6 Cooking fish fillets takes approximately 9–10 minutes per 1b at 500 watts; 7–8 minutes per 1b at 600 watts; 6–7 minutes per 1b at 650 watts.

Whole fish will take approximately 11–13 minutes per 1b at 500 watts; 8–10 minutes per 1b at 600 watts; 7–9 minutes per 1b at 650 watts.

DEEP FRYING

Although many people try to cut down on fried food, this is one of the most traditional and delicious ways to eat some fish. It is especially suited to small fish, such as whitebait, sprats and fish fillets, and it is a popular way to cook scampi.

1 Food must be coated before frying to provide a crisp outside and to prevent the fish breaking up and the fat soaking through.

2 Pre-heat the fat to *325–375°F*, depending on the size of the fish. It is essential to have hot oil to seal the coating and prevent soggy oily fish.

3 To test for correct frying temperature without a thermostat use a cube of stale bread: drop into the fat and it should rise to the surface crisp and evenly browned in 1 minute if the temperature is correct.

4 There are many safe and useful electric fryers on the market with temperature controls which remove the guesswork from frying.

5 If using a deep fat frying pan with a basket, care must be taken to avoid accidents. The pan should be filled to less than two-thirds full. Do not allow naked flames to lick up the sides of the pan. Should an accident occur and the fat catch fire, do not use water to douse the flames, but cover immediately with a metal lid to exclude the air and turn off the heat immediately. Try not to lift the pan.

METHODS OF COOKING FISH

STEAMING

This method of cooking fish makes it light and easy to digest. It is an excellent way to cook food for babies, convalescents and anyone with a digestive problem or who is on a light diet.

1 Fillets can be rolled or pieces placed between two plates over steadily simmering water. Otherwise use a steaming saucepan or a pressure cooker.

2 With the pressure cooker follow the manufacturers directions for best results.

POACHING

This method involves cooking, usually whole fish fillets and steaks, gently in liquid.

1 Place the liquid in a frying pan or saucepan as large as the fish.

2 Milk, stock, water or wine can all be used according to the recipe, usually with herbs and seasonings. Place the prepared fish in the pan; whole fillets such as smoked haddock can be topped with small knobs of butter.

3 Poaching is done over a low heat. If the liquid is allowed to boil, the fish will lose its delicate taste and texture. The liquor left over from poaching can be used as liquid for a sauce to accompany the fish.

METHODS OF COOKING FISH

BROILING

A fast method of cooking fillets of fish, fish steaks, cutlets and small whole fish. To save extra washing up it is advisable to line the broiler with foil, and to prevent the fish sticking to the wire rack, brush with oil before starting to cook.

1 Pre-heat the broiler and brush the fish with melted butter or oil. Whole fish should have several cuts made in the skin to allow the heat to penetrate evenly.

2 Season and place the fish in the broiler. After 1 minute, lower heat to medium. Most average-sized fish or cutlets will take about 8–10 minutes.

EN PAPILLOTE

This means cooking food in a paper case in the oven. It is especially good for whole fish and steaks as all the goodness and flavour are sealed in the parcel. The added advantage is that there is no messy pan to clean.

1 The fish can be enclosed in a buttered piece of waxed greaseproof paper though most people use foil for 'parcel' cooking now.

2 It is an ideal method of cooking for slimmers as the fish is simply sprinkled with lemon juice; herbs and seasoning and cooked in its own juice.

SHALLOW FRYING

Shallow frying, which is sometimes known as sautéing, covers the method of cooking the fish in a frying pan in a shallow layer of oil or fat.

1 Coat the food in either flour or egg and crumbs, as in deep frying.

2 The food will require turning and looking after constantly to obtain an overall even golden-brown and crisp appearance.

BECHAMEL SAUCE

A good béchamel enhances any dish requiring a white sauce and is well worth the extra few minutes it takes to prepare.

Makes 2½ cups/1 pt sauce

2½ cups/1 pt milk

1 small peeled onion, quartered

1 bay leaf

a few peppercorns

1 blade of mace

1 stalk parsley

6–7 tbsp/1½–1¾ oz butter, depending on thickness required

3–3½ tbsp/1½–1¾ oz flour, depending on thickness required

salt and white pepper

1 Place the milk in a saucepan with the onion, bay leaf, peppercorns, mace and parsley. Cover and allow to heat up on a low heat for about 10 minutes without boiling. Remove from the heat and allow to stand for a further 10 minutes covered. Strain and set aside.

2 Make the roux (a liaison of butter and flour) by melting the butter in a saucepan – do not allow to brown. Add the flour and mix well over a low heat.

3 Gradually add the strained milk and continue stirring until creamy and thick, season to taste.

In some fish dishes half or all of the milk is substituted by using the liquid in which the fish has been baked or poached.

Sauce made with a stock or stock and wine is known as a velouté sauce.

FISH STOCK

To make a good fish stock, add fish trimmings to the Court-Bouillon opposite leaving out the vinegar. The vegetables should not be simmered for longer than 30 minutes, or the stock will become bitter.

Note After fish has been cooked in the Court-Bouillon, the liquid becomes a fish stock.

COURT-BOUILLON

Used for cooking salmon, trout, crawfish and lobster

To cook 6 lb fish
10 cups/4 pt water
2 tsp salt
2 cups/8 oz carrots, peeled and sliced
2 cups/8 oz onions, peeled and sliced
¼ cup/1 oz parsley stalks
4 tbsp white wine or white wine vinegar
2 bouquets garnis or 2 bay leaves
sprigs of thyme
6 slightly crushed peppercorns

1 Place all the ingredients except the peppercorns in a fish kettle or large saucepan. Bring the liquid to the boil and skim.

2 Simmer for approximately 3–5 minutes then add the crushed peppercorns, continue simmering for a further 10–20 minutes. Allow to cool and strain through a fine sieve.

3 Use as required. After cooking fish in the court-bouillon the stock can be used several times if strained each time.

To store, pour into a plastic bag set in bowl or plastic box and freeze until cooking fish again.

The bag may be taken out when frozen and sealed. This quantity is for large fish (weighing about 6 lb) and may be halved for smaller quantities.

MORNAY SAUCE

Makes approximately 2½ cups/1 pt
2½ cups/1 pt béchamel sauce
2 egg yolks
4 tbsp cream
½ cup/2 oz grated cheese

1 Place 4 tbsp béchamel sauce in a small bowl and mix with the egg yolks and cream.

2 Add this mixture to the béchamel sauce and cook over a low heat, stirring well.

3 Gradually add grated cheese. Parmesan is ideal but individual taste can decide on the type of cheese.

Can be served with poached or steamed fillets or cutlets.

CHAUDFROID SAUCE

Makes 2½ cups/1 pt
2 cups/¾ pt béchamel sauce
⅝ cup/¼ pt aspic
1 rounded tsp gelatine
2 tbsp boiling water

1 Allow the bechamel sauce to cool but cover with plastic wrap to avoid a skin forming.

2 Make up the aspic in a jug and sprinkle the gelatine onto the hot water. Make sure the mixture is dissolved by placing the jug in a saucepan of boiling water. Allow to cool before using to coat fish fillets, small fish or steaks.

Makes $1\frac{3}{4}$ cups/$\frac{1}{2}$ pt
$\frac{3}{4}$ cup/6 oz butter
2 tbsp water
6 slightly crushed peppercorns
1 tbsp white wine vinegar
2 egg yolks
1 tbsp lemon juice
salt to taste

1 Make the sauce in an ovenproof bowl over a saucepan of hot water. If using the latter method make sure that the bottom of the bowl is not touching the hot water or the sauce will set on the bottom of the bowl before it is cooked.

2 Place the water, crushed peppercorns and white wine vinegar in a small saucepan and reduce to about 1 tbsp liquid. Set aside.

3 Cut the butter into pieces and soften gently in a small saucepan. Remove from heat.

4 Whisk the egg yolks, reduced liquid and a little of the butter in the saucepan. When the mixture becomes creamy and slightly thick, pour in the butter in a thin stream, whisking briskly. Add lemon juice and a little salt, and taste for seasoning.

5 Remove from the heat immediately it is thick. Should the sauce look as if it is curdling, add a few drops of cold water and whisk briskly for a few more minutes. This sauce can be made in a blender or food processor, but you may find that less butter will be absorbed. The addition of 1 tbsp cold water with the lemon juice will prevent it becoming too thick.

Hollandaise is served hot with broiled fish such as salmon, turbot, halibut and sea bream.

BEARNAISE SAUCE

Add another teaspoon of vinegar and some tarragon to the ingredients in step 2 for Hollandaise Sauce before reducing. The flavor of béarnaise is altogether more piquant and the end result should be slightly thicker than hollandaise with 1 tbsp chopped tarragon and 1 tbsp chopped chervil added. If these are unobtainable, use 2 tsp dried tarragon and 1 tbsp fresh chopped parsley.

MOUSSELINE SAUCE

Add 4 tbsp whipped cream to the Hollandaise Sauce as it cools and the resulting mousseline sauce can be served cold with fish or vegetables.

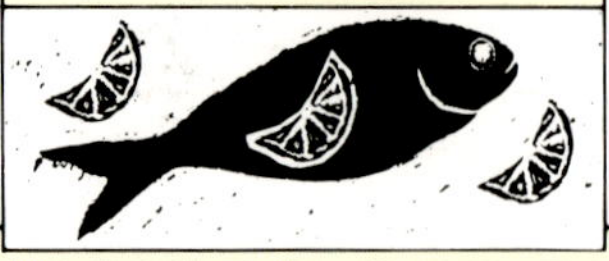

TOMATO SAUCE

Makes approximately 2½ cups/1 pt

2 tbsp oil

1 large onion, peeled and diced

1–2 cloves garlic, crushed

1 stalk celery, scrubbed

1 carrot, scraped and grated

1½ cups/14-oz can tomatoes

1½ cups/1 lb fresh tomatoes, skinned and chopped

1 bouquet garni

2 bay leaves

1 tbsp chopped fresh basil, or 1 tsp dried basil

1 tsp dried basil

parsley sprig

½ tsp sugar

salt and freshly ground black pepper

1¼ cups/½ pt fish or chicken stock

2 tbsp red wine

1 Heat the oil in a saucepan. Cook the garlic and onions over a low heat for about 4 minutes until transparent.

2 Remove the strings from the celery stalk and chop into small pieces, then add to the onion and garlic for the last 2 minutes.

3 Add all the other ingredients, bring to the boil and simmer for 40 minutes on a low heat.

4 Remove the sprig of parsley, bay leaf and bouquet garni and serve as cooked, or the sauce may be partially blended if a smoother texture is preferred.

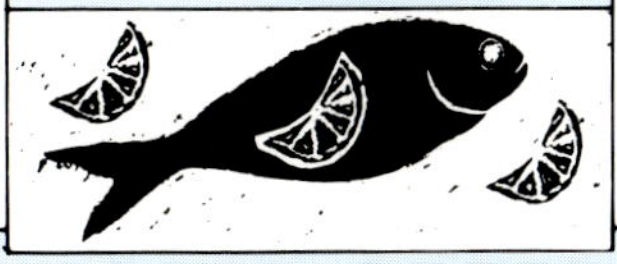

GARLIC BUTTER
4 tbsp/2 oz butter
1–2 cloves garlic, crushed
2 tsp fresh parsley, chopped

1 Cream the butter and add the well crushed garlic. Blend well. Parsley is optional but gives a better flavor to the butter.

2 Chill well.

ANCHOVY BUTTER
6 anchovy fillets
2 tbsp milk
6 tbsp/3 oz butter
pepper
1 drop tabasco sauce

1 Soak all the anchovy fillets in milk. Mash in a bowl with a wooden spoon until creamy.

2 Cream all ingredients together and chill.

MUSTARD BUTTER
4 tbsp/2 oz butter
1 tbsp French mustard
salt and pepper

Cream all ingredients together and chill.

LEMON TARRAGON BUTTER
4 tbsp/2 oz butter
juice of ½ lemon
salt and pepper
fresh tarragon or 1 tsp dried

Cream all ingredients together and chill.

CLAM CHOWDER

Serves 4
1–2 dozen clams or 1 can clams
$\frac{5}{8}$ cup/$\frac{1}{4}$ pt white wine
$1\frac{1}{4}$ cups/$\frac{1}{2}$ pt water
1 bay leaf
1 bouquet garni
$\frac{2}{3}$ cup/4 oz bacon
2 tbsp/1 oz butter
1 medium onion, diced
2 leeks, washed and chopped
1 green pepper, deseeded, blanched and diced
1 stalk celery, diced
1 small/4 oz potato, diced
salt and freshly ground pepper
few sprigs fresh thyme or $\frac{1}{2}$ tsp dried thyme
4–6 fresh tomatoes, skinned or $1\frac{1}{2}$ cups/15-oz can tomatoes
1 tbsp chopped parsley
8 plain crackers, crushed

1 Poach the fresh clams for about 5 minutes in the white wine and water with a bay leaf and bouquet garni added. If using canned, poach for 10 minutes.

2 Cut the bacon into small pieces. Melt the butter in a saucepan and add bacon. After about 2 minutes add the onion, leeks, diced pepper, diced celery and diced potato. Sweat the vegetables for about 6 minutes then add the clam liquor with seasoning, thyme and chopped tomatoes. Make liquid up to approximately $1\frac{1}{2}$ pt with water. Bring the soup to the boil, reduce heat and simmer until the vegetables are tender.

3 Add the clams a few minutes before serving.

Serve the chowder sprinkled with crushed crackers and parsley.

FISH CHOWDER

Serves 4

1 lb white fish, boned
2 tbsp/1 oz butter
1 large onion, peeled and finely diced
1–2 cloves garlic, peeled and crushed
4 potatoes, peeled and diced
$1\frac{1}{2}$ cups/14-oz can tomatoes
few sprigs of thyme
few sprigs of parsley
1–2 bay leaves or 1 bouquet garni
salt and freshly ground black pepper
pinch of cayenne pepper
$1\frac{1}{4}$ cups/$\frac{1}{2}$ pt hot water
$\frac{5}{8}$ cup/$\frac{1}{4}$ pt milk
8 plain crackers, crushed
1 tbsp chopped parsley

Use whiting, haddock or any leftover raw fish.

1 Make sure the fish is boned as far as possible, as most people object to fish bones. Cut into even-sized pieces.

2 Melt the butter and sweat the onion, crushed garlic and diced potatoes for about 5 minutes.

3 Add the can of tomatoes with the herbs and seasoning. Pour in the hot water.

4 Bring to the boil and simmer for about 20 minutes, or until potatoes are cooked. Add the fish for about the last 10 minutes of cooking. Taste for seasoning and make sure all the fish is cooked.

5 Add the milk and stir over a low heat for a few minutes.

6 Place the crackers in the bottom of the soup bowls and pour over the soup. Sprinkle with chopped parsley.

Serve with warm French bread or crispy rolls.

Fish chowder

SMOKED SALMON APPETIZER

Serves 4

4 oz smoked salmon pieces
2 tbsp fresh parsley, chopped
freshly ground black pepper
juice of 2 lemons
¼ cup/1 oz cream cheese
2 tbsp double or whipping cream

1 Select a few small pieces of smoked salmon and retain for garnish. Pound, sieve or blend the remainder, then add a good shake of black pepper and lemon juice and mix well.

2 Add the smoked salmon and chopped parsley to the cream cheese and double or whipping cream. Mix well.

3 This mixture can be piped on crackers or toast as canapés decorated with small curls of smoked salmon or served in small ramekins as an appetizer with triangles of toast.

SMOKED MACKEREL CREAM

Serves 4

1 large/10 oz smoked mackerel fillet
juice of 1 lemon
1 clove garlic, crushed
2 tbsp vegetable or olive oil
¼ cup/1 oz cream cheese
2 tbsp parsley, finely chopped
salt and freshly ground pepper

To garnish

1 lemon cut into wedges

1 Remove the skin from the mackerel and check for any bones which may be left. Mash in a bowl with a fork. Sprinkle with the lemon juice.

2 Mix the crushed garlic, oil and cream cheese in a bowl.

3 Gradually add the fish and the parsley. Season well. Serve in small ramekins.

Alternatively feed the ingredients into a food processor and mix for a few seconds.

4 Serve with triangles of brown toast and lemon wedges.

TARAMASALATA

Serves 4–6
8 oz smoked cod's roe
3–4 tbsp lemon juice
1 cup/3 oz boiled potato, sieved
1 slice white bread, crustless
1–2 cloves garlic, crushed
3 tbsp olive oil
1–3 tsp cold water
salt and white pepper
To garnish
12 black olives
sprig of parsley

1 Remove the skin from the cod's roe, carefully scooping away all the flesh. Place in a bowl and sprinkle with 2 tbsp of lemon juice. Mix well with a wooden spoon. Add the sieved potato a bit at a time.

2 Steep the slice of bread in cold water and squeeze dry with one hand. Cream into the fish mixture. Add finely crushed garlic and either one or two cloves, according to individual taste.

3 Beat in the oil a few drops at a time, then gradually add cold water until a thick creamy consistency is reached. Season with white pepper and a little salt (cod's roe can be salty, so taste as seasoning progresses). More lemon juice can be added, if needed.

4 Alternatively feed the oil and garlic into a food processor or large blender and gradually add the other ingredients. The taramasalata will be made in a few minutes. Add cold water at the end to achieve the correct creamy consistency.

5 Garnish with black olives and a sprig of parsley and serve with crisp toast or hot pita bread.

AVOCADO WITH SHRIMPS IN SEAFOOD SAUCE

Serves 4
2 ripe avocados
lemon juice
3⁄4 cup/4 oz peeled shrimps
5⁄8 cup/1⁄4 pt Seafood Sauce
To garnish
parsley or watercress
4 shrimps in their shells

1 Cut the avocados lengthwise with a sharp stainless steel knife and carefully remove the stone. Scoop out some of the flesh from each half and chop into small pieces. Place in a bowl and sprinkle with lemon juice.

2 Add the shrimps, making sure they are defrosted, and drained if using frozen, to the seafood sauce. Mix well with the chopped avocado and taste for seasoning. Return to the avocado skins.

3 Garnish with watercress or parsley. Add one or two shrimps in shells at the narrow end of the avocado half if liked.

FISH SAVOURIES WITH SPICY TOMATO SAUCE

Serves 4

8 oz fish, cooked
2 tbsp/1 oz butter
1 small onion, peeled and sliced
2½ cups/8 oz potatoes, cooked and sieved
2 drops tabasco sauce
1 tsp tomato ketchup
salt and freshly ground pepper
1 tbsp chopped parsley
1 egg, beaten
dried breadcrumbs
oil for frying
⅝ cup/¼ pt Spicy Tomato Sauce

Leftover poached salmon, trout or canned fish such as tuna or salmon can be used.

1 Make sure that all the bones are removed from the cooked fish.

2 Melt the butter and sweat the onion until tender. Add the potatoes, seasoning and parsley to the onion in a bowl, and finally add the fish and mix well.

3 Mix with a little of the beaten egg. Add a few drops of water to the remaining egg. Flour the hands and form the mixture into small balls and chill in the refrigerator.

4 Roll the fish balls in the egg, and water mixture, and then in the dried crumbs.

5 Fry the balls in deep fat or in a frying pan one-third filled with oil which has been heated.

6 Serve on a plate. Spear the balls with wooden cocktail sticks or toothpicks and serve around a dish of hot spicy tomato sauce. Can be served with drinks or at buffet parties.

BAKED AVOCADO WITH CRAB

Serves 4

2 ripe avocados

7-oz can of crab meat or
the meat from 1 cooked crab

1 tbsp lemon juice

2 tbsp white wine

few drops of tabasco sauce

2 tsp tomato purée (paste)

salt and freshly ground pepper

$1\frac{1}{4}$ cups/$\frac{1}{2}$ pt Béchamel Sauce

To garnish

1 tbsp parsley, finely chopped

Oven temperature 350°F

1 Cut the avocados in half carefully and remove the stones and some of the flesh.

2 Sprinkle the crab meat and chopped avocado flesh with lemon juice and white wine.

3 Add the rest of the ingredients to the béchamel sauce and fill the halved avocados, piling the mixture up as high as it will go without spilling.

4 Bake in a moderate oven until golden brown. Serve sprinkled with chopped parsley.

This dish can be made with tuna fish in place of crab.

AVOCADO, GRAPEFRUIT AND SHRIMP SALAD

Serves 4
2 grapefruit
2 avocados
1½ cups/8 oz prawns or shrimps
⅝ cup/¼ pt French dressing or Seafood Sauce

1 To make the grapefruit sections, place the fruit in a bowl and pour boiling water on top to cover. Leave for 2 minutes, then remove and allow to cool. Cut a slice from the top of the fruit, then cut the peel and pith off in strips to reveal the flesh. It is essential to use a small sharp knife.

2 When all the pith has been cut away, remove each section by cutting between the membranes of each segment. At the end only the tough outer skin should be left and each section of fruit is separate without skin.

3 Peel the avocados, cut in half lengthways and remove the stones. Cut the flesh into slices.

4 Arrange the avocado slices, grapefruit segments and shrimps in dishes and serve with French dressing, Seafood Sauce or Mayonnaise as preferred. The dressing may be poured over the salad or served separately.

POACHED SALMON

Serves 8–10
7–8 lb salmon
½ lemon
½ onion
1 bay leaf
1 sprig parsley
Court-Bouillon

1 Prepare the salmon by slitting the stomach and removing the insides from head to tail. Wash the cavity under cold running water.

Place half a lemon, 2 small pieces of onion, a bay leaf and sprig of parsley in the cavity. (The fish can be gutted by removing the head and drawing the entrails out with the curved handle of a soup ladle. This means the stomach remains whole and is better to dress for a buffet table. However many fish are bought already gutted.)

2 Half fill a fish kettle with the court-bouillon and lower the fish into the cold liquid, bring to the boil gently and then simmer over a low heat for about 45 minutes. Remove from the heat and allow to cool for some hours in the fish liquid.

Do not cook over a high heat or the fish will split.

3 Remove fish from the liquid and allow to drain for about 1 hour if using cold, as a dressed salmon. Alternatively serve the salmon hot with Hollandaise or Mousseline Sauce.

ALTERNATIVE METHOD

As fish kettles are fairly large, the smallest being around 18 in, many people do not want the expense of buying one or the storage problem for an occasional large fish. It is possible to cook a fairly large fish in a modern oven if you have a large roasting pan. Pour the court-bouillon to about a quarter of the way up the pan and place the fish diagonally across. The head may be cut off and the tail wrapped in foil to make the fish fit. Cook the head beside the fish. Pour over as much liquid as the pan will take and cover with a double sheet of foil or another large roasting pan.

Allow 10 minutes for each 1 lb using this method at *325°F*. Cool as instructed above.

This method is also used for salmon, trout and sea bass.

TO DRESS A SALMON

1 poached salmon with head and tail
To garnish
2½ cups/½ pt aspic
1 cucumber
12 stuffed olives
2 lemons
watercress

1 Remove the top skin of the salmon and any grey bits on the pink flesh with the back of a knife.

2 Arrange on a serving platter. Make up the aspic jelly as directed on the packet with boiling water and allow to cool.

3 Paint the salmon over with the aspic and allow to set slightly. After about 30 minutes pour a little more aspic all over the fish. Allow to set.

4 Slice the cucumber very thinly and cut slices in half. Cut the olives into thin slices. The lemon can be marked on the outside with a sharp knife in lines and sliced thinly.

5 Arrange the cucumber slices in a wavy pattern along the edge of the fish. Use the olives to mark the backbone. Paint each slice with aspic before arranging.

Use the halved lemon slices for the other side of the fish, then pour over another coating of almost setting aspic. Any excess aspic may be chopped on the plate around the fish when it has set.

These are only suggestions, and the fish can also be decorated with radishes, hard-boiled egg, parsley, halved lemons.

6 Serve the salmon with Mayonnaise or Green Sauce.

SALMON FISH CAKES

Makes 12 fish cakes
6 cups/2 lb peeled and sliced potatoes
8 oz cooked salmon, flaked and boned
4 oz coley or haddock, cooked, flaked and boned
1 tbsp tomato catsup
1 tsp Worcestershire sauce
salt and freshly ground pepper
1 tbsp finely chopped parsley
1 egg
Coating
1 egg
2 tbsp water
¾ cup/3 oz dried breadcrumbs
Frying temperature 375°F

1 Boil the potatoes until soft, drain and mash through a ricer, a large vegetable mouli or a sieve. It is important that the potato is free from lumps.

2 Mix the flaked fish into the potatoes and gradually add seasonings and the parsley.

3 Finally bind with beaten egg.

4 Flour a board and, using a 2-in scone or cookie cutter, shape the cakes onto a tray or baking sheet. Chill in the freezer or top of the fridge for at least 30 minutes.

5 Flour the hands and dip each cake into the beaten egg mixed with the water, and then coat with the breadcrumbs. Pat the crumbs well into the cakes. Chill for a further 30 minutes.

6 Fry in deep fat for about 4-5 minutes until crisp. Serve with wedges of lemon.

The fried cakes can be refrigerated or frozen and used as required.

TROUT CHAUDFROID

Serves 4
4 trout
$1\frac{1}{4}$ cups/$\frac{1}{2}$ pt chaudfroid sauce
To garnish
cucumber peel
canned pimento
stuffed olives, sliced
watercress

1 Cook the trout 'au bleu' and allow to cool.

2 Remove the heads and top skin. Lift top fillet from fish carefully and remove the bone. Lay fillet back on the fish.

3 Coat with sauce. Garnish with cucumber peel cut into thin strips, diamond-shaped pieces of pimento, and sliced stuffed olives to make flowers and leaves. Surround head end with sprigs of watercress. An excellent summer meal or buffet dish.

TROUT 'AU BLEU'

Serves 4

$4\frac{3}{8}$ cups/$1\frac{3}{4}$ pt Court-Bouillon

$\frac{5}{8}$ cup/$\frac{1}{4}$ pt white wine vinegar

1 Gut the trout just before cooking but do not scale. Place in a saucepan.

2 Pour on white wine vinegar, add lukewarm, well-seasoned Court-Bouillon and allow to simmer for about 10 minutes. Do not allow to boil or the fish will split. Serve with lemon wedges and Hollandaise Sauce.

FILLETS OF SOLE IN WHITE WINE WITH MUSHROOMS

Serves 4
4 lemon sole, filleted
5/8 cup/1/4 pt white wine
5/8 cup/1/4 pt water
1 small onion, peeled and sliced
6 small mushrooms
1 bay leaf
sprig of parsley
4 peppercorns
1 tbsp/1/2 oz butter
2 tbsp/1/2 oz flour
2 tbsp light cream
Oven temperature 350°F

1 Roll the fillets of sole head to tail and arrange in an ovenproof dish.

2 Pour over the wine, water, onion, mushroom stalks, herbs and seasoning. Cook in a moderate oven covered with a buttered paper or foil or lid for 15–20 minutes.

3 Strain the liquid from the fish and make up to 1 1/4 cups/1/2 pt with water or wine if necessary. Poach the mushroom caps in this liquid for a few minutes – remove and keep warm.

4 Make a roux with the butter and flour and make up a sauce with the fish liquid.

5 Add the cream to the sauce just before serving, pour over the warmed fish, and serve with Duchesse potatoes, mushroom caps and sprigs of watercress.

SOLE MEUNIERE

Serves 4
2 lemon or Dover soles, filleted
½ cup/2 oz flour
4 tbsp/2 oz butter
1 tbsp fresh parsley, chopped
1 lemon

1 Flour the fillets of sole and shake off excess.

2 Melt the butter and shallow fry the fillets for about 3 minutes either side.

3 Arrange the fillets on a warm serving dish and keep warm.

4 Add the parsley to the butter in the pan. Add a little extra butter if necessary.

Pour over the fish and serve with wedges of lemon.

SOLE DUGLERE

Serves 4

4 tbsp/2 oz butter

1 onion, peeled and chopped

3 tomatoes, peeled and chopped

8 fillets of sole

salt and freshly ground pepper

5/8 cup/1/4 pt white wine

2 tbsp/1/2 oz flour

To garnish

1 tomato, peeled and sliced

few sprigs of parsley

1 Melt 2 tbsp/1 oz butter in a frying pan and add the chopped onions. Sweat over a low heat for a few minutes. Add the tomatoes and simmer for a further 2 minutes.

2 Fold the fish in three and lay on top of the tomato and onion mixture, add seasoning and white wine and simmer for a further 12 minutes.

3 Remove the fish to a serving dish and keep warm. Reduce the sauce by about half over a medium heat.

4 Make a roux with the remaining butter and flour. Add the sieved liquid to make a sauce. Arrange the sole on a plate with Duchesse potatoes and mask with the sauce.

Garnish with sliced tomatoes and sprigs of parsley.

SKATE IN CAPER SAUCE

Serves 4

4 wings of skate

1¼ cups/½ pt water

1 tbsp vinegar

1 small onion, peeled and sliced

1 bay leaf

salt and freshly ground pepper

1 tbsp/½ oz butter

2 tbsp/½ oz flour

3 tbsp capers, chopped

2 tbsp fresh parsley, chopped

Oven temperature 350°F

1 Place the skate wings in a baking dish and pour over the water, vinegar, sliced onion and bay leaf. Season with salt and pepper.

2 Cook covered in the oven for about 15–20 minutes.

3 In a saucepan make a roux with the butter and flour to make up a sauce with 1¼ cups/½ pt of the fish liquor, strained from the skate. Add the chopped capers and parsley.

Pour the sauce over the fish and serve with sauté potatoes and a crisp green vegetable.

If skate is unavailable use halibut or turbot.

RED MULLET PROVENCAL

Serves 2
4 red mullet
2 tbsp/1 oz butter
1¼ cups/½ pt Tomato Sauce
1 green/or red pepper, deseeded and diced
1 tbsp port or sherry
salt and freshly ground pepper
stoned black olives
To garnish
lemon wedges
4 anchovy fillets
Oven temperature 350°F

1 Rub the fish with melted butter and place under a hot broiler for 2 minutes each side.

2 Arrange in an ovenproof dish.

3 Mix the tomato sauce with the diced pepper and the port. Season the fish well and pour over the sauce, then arrange the olives.

4 Bake for 20 minutes. Serve hot, garnished with lemon wedges and anchovy fillets, or serve chilled as an hors d'oeuvre.

Red mullet or rouget as it is known in France has a very delicate taste and is best prepared simply either by broiling or baking in foil. It has no gall and does not need to be cleaned; indeed the liver is considered a delicacy.

FISH KABOBS ON RICE WITH SPICY TOMATO SAUCE

Serves 4

2 thick cod steaks
8 medium mushrooms
8 bay leaves
8 cooked shrimps
1 green pepper, deseeded
1 red or yellow pepper, deseeded
2 zucchini, thickly sliced

Marinade

4 tbsp oil
6 tbsp lemon juice
salt and freshly ground pepper
1 tbsp roughly chopped parsley
1 bay leaf
1 small onion, thinly sliced in rings
½ tsp paprika
1¼ cups/8 oz long grain rice, uncooked
½ tsp turmeric

To garnish

lemon wedges
parsley sprigs

1 Cut the cod steaks into 12 even-sized pieces and thread onto the skewers one piece at a time. Alternate with mushrooms, bay leaves, shrimps, squares of blanched pepper and slices of zucchini.

2 Make up the marinade and pour over the fish. Leave to marinade for at least 3 hours and turn the kabobs from time to time.

3 Add 4 cups of water with turmeric added to the rice and cook as directed on the packet or see Paella.

4 Paint the broiler rack with oil to prevent food sticking and broil the skewered food for about 4 minutes each side until the cod is cooked. Serve on a warm bed of rice with Spicy Tomato Sauce and a crisp green salad.

SALAD NICOISE

Serves 4

2 large/1 lb potatoes, boiled
2 cups/8 oz green beans, fresh or frozen
7-oz can tuna fish
5/8 cup/1/4 pt vinaigrette
4 tomatoes, skinned and sliced
1/4 cucumber
2 hard-boiled eggs
12 black or green olives, stones removed
6 anchovy fillets, cut into thin slices

To garnish

small cherry tomatoes

1 Cook the potatoes in their skins until tender. Remove the skins and dice finely. Cook the beans in a small amount of boiling water for about 6 minutes. Frozen beans can be used; cook as directed on the packet.

2 Mix the potatoes, beans and half the tuna fish with three-quarters of the vinaigrette.

3 Arrange the sliced tomatoes on the bottom and around the bowl, arrange thinly sliced cucumber on top, and sprinkle with a little vinaigrette. Place a few chunks of tuna fish on the tomato and cucumber.

4 The eggs may be cut into slices or wedges and can be used on top as a garnish or arranged to make a bed for the beans, potatoes and tuna fish mixture.

5 Arrange the fish mixture in the middle and arrange the anchovies in a diamond-shaped pattern on the beans, decorating each space with an olive. Pour over any remaining dressing.

This makes a delicious lunch, appetizer for dinner party or buffet salad, with crispy French bread.

TUNA-STUFFED POTATOES

Serves 4

4 large potatoes, scrubbed

4 tomatoes, skinned and chopped

4 spring (green) onions, washed and chopped

4 tbsp sour cream

salt and freshly ground pepper

scant cup/ 7-oz can tuna fish, in oil

Oven temperature 350°F

1 Make a cross on the potato skins and bake for 1 hour or until cooked.

2 Halve the potatoes and scoop out the cooked potato, retaining the skins.

3 Mix all ingredients together, season well and arrange in the potato skins.

4 Re-heat before serving.

Tuna-stuffed potatoes

STUFFED BAKED MACKEREL

Serves 4

4 mackerel

salt and freshly ground pepper

2 tbsp lemon juice

4 tbsp oil

1 medium onion

¾–1 cup/ 4 oz gooseberries, fresh or canned

4 level tbsp breadcrumbs

1 tbsp chopped parsley

1 tsp chopped mint

salt and freshly ground pepper

2 tbs/1 oz butter

To garnish

wedges of lemon

Oven temperature 400°F reducing to 350°F

1 Clean the fish, remove head, slit down the stomach and remove backbone. Sprinkle with salt, pepper and a little of the lemon juice.

2 Heat 2 tbsp oil and fry finely chopped onions, then add the gooseberries and mix well.

3 Mix breadcrumbs, parsley, mint, lemon juice and seasoning together, add onion and gooseberries and mix well.

4 Stuff into mackerel and secure edges together with a cocktail stick or toothpick.

5 Place fish in remaining oil in a casserole, dot with butter and bake in a hot oven for 15 minutes then reduce heat and cook for a further 15–20 minutes until fish is tender.

LOBSTER

To prepare and cook a live lobster. Take a skewer or sharp knife and drive through the cross which is on the head. Grip the lobster firmly behind the head and plunge into a large saucepan of boiling salted water. A bay leaf, sprig of parsley or bouquet garni may be added. Cook for 15 minutes for each 1 lb of lobster. Allow to cool in the liquid. Leave the antennae on the lobster as they form part of the decoration if serving in the shell. When cool, twist off the claws, retaining small claws for garnish.

DRESSED LOBSTER

1 Crack the pincer claws with a small hammer and take out the meat with a skewer.

2 Cut the lobster lengthways from head to tail using a sharp knife. Remove the stomach bag on the right side of the head and remove the grey spongy parts known as 'dead man's fingers'.

3 Remove the coral, wash and retain for decoration.

4 Now remove all the meat from the shell. Keep the green liver meat which is edible.

5 Flavor the meat with lemon juice and seasoning or mayonnaise and return to the shell. Serve on a platter of lettuce.

Lobsters are best at about $1\frac{3}{4}$–$2\frac{1}{2}$ lb as this will give two good servings or about $\frac{3}{4}$ lb meat. A well cooked lobster will feel heavy and the tail should be curled under the body.

Shrimps have become a general term for several kinds of shellfish. They are usually sold cooked and are widely available frozen.

MOULES MARINIERE

Serves 4
approx 4 lb mussels
4 tbsp/2 oz butter
1 medium onion, finely chopped
1–2 cloves of garlic, finely crushed
1¼ cups/½ pt white wine
1 bay leaf
fresh sprigs parsley
2 tbsp chopped parsley, optional
2 tbsp cream, optional

1 Make sure the mussels are properly prepared before cooking. They should be alive – tap with a wooden spoon and if any remain open discard at once. Wash and scrub the shells thoroughly under a cold running tap and remove the beard. Place in a bowl of cold water and change the water several times to remove the sand.

2 Heat butter in a very large saucepan or frying pan. Add the chopped onion and garlic. Allow to sweat gently in the butter without browning.

3 Add the wine, bay leaf and sprigs of parsley. Turn up the heat and add the cleaned mussels. Shake over the heat for about 6–10 minutes until all the mussels are open.

Discard any mussels which do not open. Divide the mussels into serving bowls and if liked add the cream and the parsley to the juice. Heat for a further minute and pour over the mussels.

Serve with warm French bread and extra plates for empty shells.

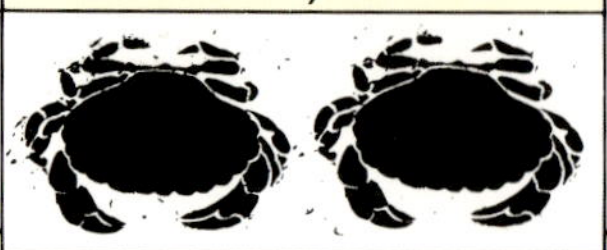

SHELLFISH QUICHE

Serves 4–6
Shortcrust Pastry
1½ cups/6 oz flour
4 tbsp/2 oz butter or hard margarine
3 tbsp/1½ oz hard white cooking fat
1 egg yolk
few drops water
Filling
1 large or 3 medium tomatoes, skinned
few leaves of basil, chopped or ½ tsp dried basil
¾ cup/4 oz prawns, shrimps, crab or lobster meat, fresh or canned
3 eggs
⅝ cup/¼ pt double or whipping cream
salt and freshly ground white pepper
Oven temperature 400°F reducing to 325°F

1 Make up the pastry by sieving the flour into a bowl with the salt and add the fat to the flour in small pea-sized pieces. Rub in the fat until the mixture resembles fine breadcrumbs. Make a well in the center of the mixture and add the egg yolk and 2–3 drops of water. Mix with a spatula and if it appears too dry, add a further 2 or 3 drops of water gradually (remember you can always add but not take out if the pastry is too wet). Knead lightly with your hand and the bowl should be clean and the pastry a firm smooth dough. Rest in the fridge for about 20 minutes.

2 Meanwhile prepare an 8-in pie plate on a baking sheet or use a china quiche dish. Cut a piece of waxed paper slightly larger than the dish and have some dried beans such as kidney or haricot which can be kept for baking pastry ready for use.

3 Lightly flour the work top and roll out the pastry to fit the dish about ¼ in thick and about ½ in bigger than the quiche. Lift the pastry on the rolling pin and ease onto the dish. Run the rolling pin over the top of the dish to remove the pastry evenly.

4 Line with paper and baking beans and bake for 20 minutes. Reduce heat after quiche is removed from the oven.

5 Slice the tomatoes, place on the bottom of the pie plate and sprinkle with basil. Spread the shellfish over the tomatoes.

6 Mix the eggs with the cream, season and pour into the prepared dish.

7 Return to the middle shelf in the oven until set and pale golden. Garnish with fresh watercress.

Alternatively make in individual tart pans for a first course or snack meal.

SMOKED SALMON QUICHE

Substitute 4 oz chopped smoked salmon pieces for shellfish. Asparagus may be used in place of tomato. Omit basil.

DRESSED CRAB

Serves 2

1 crab, cooked

2 tbsp white breadcrumbs

1–2 tbsp Mayonnaise

½ tsp French mustard

salt and freshly ground pepper

juice of ½ lemon

To garnish

fresh parsley, finely chopped

paprika pepper

1 egg, hard-boiled

lettuce

1 Place the cooked crab on a board and twist the claws until they separate from the body. Crack the claws open with a hammer. Take a skewer and remove the white meat from the claws and place in a bowl.

2 Take hold of the crab firmly with two hands and with the thumbs push the body section away from the shell.

3 Take out and discard the following: the small sac or stomach bag which is attached to the large shell, any green tinged material in the large shell and lastly, the grey spongy parts known as 'dead man's fingers'.

4 Scrape the brownish meat from the shell into a second bowl.

5 Cut the body into two and scrape any white meat left into the first bowl.

6 Tap the shell to remove the ragged sharp edge. Wash and scrub the inside and outside of the shell thoroughly and rinse well (do not use soap).

7 Dry off the shell and brush with some olive oil.

8 Mix the white breadcrumbs with the brown meat and cream well with the mayonnaise, French mustard and seasonings.

9 Arrange the white meat mixed with lemon juice and salt and pepper on each side of the shell and the brown meat down the middle.

10 Garnish with rows of chopped parsley, paprika and the separately sieved white and yolk of egg.

Arrange by placing the garnish on the edge of the spatula. Serve on a bed of lettuce surrounded by small claws, with thinly sliced wholewheat bread and butter. Serve mayonnaise separately.

SCALLOPS

The scallop is a bivalve shellfish which is easily recognized by the familiar fan-shaped shell. It is also well known by its French name, Coquille Saint-Jacques.

It is useful to obtain the shells when buying scallops as they are ideal for serving scallop recipes. The fish shop will prepare the scallops by removing the inedible parts and the beards. However, if you are using the shells to serve the fish, remove the scallops and scrub the shells inside and out with a stiff brush to remove all traces of shell crust. Do not use soap but rinse well in cold water, after scrubbing. To re-use the shells, it is advisable to clean well and bring to the boil in a saucepan of water and then allow to dry and store in a plastic bag.

SCALLOPS AU GRATIN

Serves 4

8–16 scallops, depending on size
2–4 tbsp/1–2 oz butter
1 small onion, peeled and finely chopped or 6 spring (green) onions, cleaned and chopped
1 clove garlic, crushed (optional)
5/8 cup/1/4 pt white wine
5/8 cup/1/4 pt fish stock or water
1 bay leaf
1 bouquet garni
salt and freshly ground pepper
1 1/2 tbsp/3/4 oz butter
3 tbsp/3/4 oz flour
1–2 tbsp light cream
2 tbsp fresh breadcrumbs, dried
1 tbsp parmesan cheese

1 Cut the scallops into slices. Melt the butter in a saucepan.

2 Sweat the onion and garlic over a low heat for about 3 minutes.

3 Add the sliced scallops, cook for a further 1 minute and then add the wine and water or fish stock with the bay leaf and bouquet garni. Season well.

4 Bring to the boil and turn the heat down low and simmer for about 6 minutes. Allow to cool.

5 Strain the liquor from the scallops, retaining the vegetables. Discard the bay leaf and bouquet garni.

6 Pipe a border of mashed potatoes around 8 deep, cleaned scallop shells.

7 Make a roux with the butter and flour, make a sauce with the fish liquor. Taste for seasoning, add cream.

8 Add the onion mixture, then the scallops to the sauce and divide the mixture between the shells.

9 Sprinkle with a mixture of breadcrumbs and parmesan cheese. Brown in a hot oven or in the broiler.

If using 8 scallops, you will only need 4 shells and 1 tbsp cream. One shell is sufficient for a fish course but 2 will be needed for a main course.

PAELLA

Serves 4

1 lb cod or halibut

2½ cups/1 pt Court-Bouillon

4 tbsp oil

2 cloves garlic, crushed

3 medium onions, peeled

1¾ cups/12 oz long grain rice

pinch of saffron or ¼ tsp turmeric

2½ cups/1 pt fish or chicken stock

1 red pepper, deseeded

1 green pepper, deseeded

⅝ cup/¼ pt white wine and water

1½ pt mussels

1 generous cup/6 oz peeled shrimps

To garnish

wedges of lemon

1 tbsp parsley, chopped

4–8 large cooked shrimps (optional)

1 Poach the cod in 1 pt court-bouillon for 5 minutes.

2 Put the oil in a large pan and sweat the garlic and 2 of the onions, one thinly sliced and the other finely chopped, for about 4 minutes without browning.

3 Add the rice to the pan and stir over the heat for a few minutes until rice just begins to color.

4 Strain the cod and retain the stock. Add saffron or turmeric to the stock and pour over the rice, stirring from time to time over a low heat. Cook covered with a lid or foil for the first 10 minutes.

5 Blanch the peppers for 2 minutes then dice finely, add to the rice and stir well.

6 In another saucepan, place the other finely chopped onion with water and wine mixture and a good shake of pepper. Bring to the boil and add the cleaned mussels. Cook for 10 minutes until steamed open.

7 Add the strained mussel liquor to the rice and stir well. Cook for a further 5 minutes or until tender.

8 Add chunks of white fish, shrimps and mussels.

Serve piping hot sprinkled with parsley and garnished with lemon wedges.